METAPHORS MOANS AND MORE

―――

Karmel Poet

Metaphors Moans and More
Copyright © 2015 by Karmel Poet

Cover Art by: G Troy Pope

All rights reserved. No part of this book may be reproduced or transmitted in any form or by any means without written permission from the author.

ISBN (978-0-9973435-0-2)

Table of Contents

Dream 5

My Head 7

My Pace 9

Next Time 10

Can't Help Myself 11

Kiss and Tell 15

Round One 18

Nature 22

Men or Frogs 23

Quickie 25

Happy Birthday 27

Don't Bite Your Tongue 31

Imagination 33

Round Two 36

Thanks 39

At the Altar 41

After Dinner Surprise 43

More Than A Freak 46

Tonight 48

Your Wife 51

Round Three 53

Show Me 56
The Stroll 58
New Toy 60
Breaking Point 62
Inhibitions 65
The Story of We 66
Round Four 67
Regale Me.. 71
Next Best Thing 73
A Hard Day 75
Magnify 79
Neighbors 80
Round Five 85
Stop Frontin' 87
Heat 89
The Recipe... 91
Forbidden Pleasure 92
Knocked Out 95
Be My 98

Dream

Laying here listening to slow jams
All alone
No one to hold me
But
Not for long
He's on his way to spend the night
To take the wrongs and make them right
I put him off
I played the game
Tonight I'm ready to make him say my name
I've played innocent long enough
Tonight I'm ready to show him my stuff
Not too much
Not the first time
Just enough to make him glad he's mine
I hear his car in the drive and start to grin
The resistance is over
Tonight I'm giving in
He knocks on the door
He doesn't have a key
He may tomorrow
If he pleases me
I opened the door with a smile
Stepped aside
I let him know with one glance he was in for a hell of a ride
He returned my look

Adding his own little smirk
Letting me know that he was more than ready to go to work
This was one chocolate bar that I was ready to taste
We took care of the preliminaries
There was no time to waste
I realized that I had waited a little too long for this day
The bedroom was really too far away
I lived alone
Starting here could do no harm
So I reached for him
And
There went the alarm
I couldn't believe it
I wanted to scream
It was time to go to work
It had only been a dream
There was no use laying there I had things to do
So I got up
Hoping that
One day
My dream would come true

My Head

Just stand there for a minute
Let me see
All
That's about to be used
To please me
Those strong arms
Made to hold me against the wall
That back
I'll be scratching as your name I call
That chest
I'll be kissing as I start from your lips
Then down I go
Wait
Don't move the shorts
I'm enjoying the show
I'm getting wet just thinking about all the things that
I'm going to do to you
And all the things that we'll do together before this night is through
I know that you will give my body the pleasure that it seeks
But first
I want to see how long it takes me to make your knees weak
Let me remove those shorts
All of you needs to breathe
You keep standing right there while I get on my knees

I can tell you like watching me
That comes as no surprise
I like watching you
I want to make you close your eyes
Moan
Say my name
Pull my hair
I want to see what it takes to have you gasping for air
Or have you looking for a place to sit
Telling me that you can't take it and I need to quit
It will only get better once we finally make it to the bed
But first
Let me act out the thoughts that looking at you has put into my head

My Pace

I love the feel of the air on my skin as I move

It took me a minute

But I finally found my groove

My legs pumping in rhythm

My hands moving too

You become breathless

As I do what I do

You want to beat me

But

You can't match my pace

I just smile as the sweat drips down my face

Sometimes I switch it up

Fast then slow

I like to keep you guessing so you'll never know

From the time that I start just when I'll be done

I'm always sweaty and sore

At the end of my morning run

Next Time

It started raining
So I wanted to play
But
I knew my man had had a long day
I thought about a toy but
That wasn't enough
So I went to the room and got the handcuffs
Checked on the kids to make sure they were asleep
With the mood I was in
Things were about to get deep
Back to my bedroom for lingerie and a blindfold
Then I stood in front of the TV and said
Baby
I'm cold
He looked at the handcuffs
Looked at me
Said somebody's feeling frisky I see
I told him he'd see more than that when we got to the room because somebody was getting tied up
And I meant soon
Something I said awoke in him the sexual beast
He picked me up and growled
You're about to be my feast
I moaned and said no
You first as I
Nibbled on his ear
The way he threw me on the bed
Should've caused some fear
We wrestled with each other until we ended up in sixty-nine
I guess we'll just have to use the handcuffs next time

Can't Help Myself

I thought I could handle it

I thought I was slick

I never thought that I could be controlled by my dick

I was Mr. Feel Good

Everybody wanted me

Women would give anything just to be the one that I chose to entertain for the night

There was a part of me that knew it wasn't right

But I didn't care

I was all about that feeling

I got off on keeping the ladies reeling

Then something happened

Suddenly I stopped

I met a woman that made my heart drop

Into my stomach

At the sound of her voice

I suddenly realized that I had a choice

I could stay a whore

Or try to improve

She made me want to prove

That I could be a better man

Worthy

Of asking her for her hand

And I did get better

I must admit

But something happened

I got hit

By a bus

In the form of major stress

That I needed to release by making a mess

In my bed with my future wife

But

She had a lot going on in her life

I felt neglected and made the mistake of talking to another woman one night real late

I knew she wanted me but thought I could resist

I should've known better than to call her when I was pissed

When I get mad I get horny and she must've felt the heat

Because she took me there before I could even speak

She caught me off guard

I fell fast

I became a victim of the games of my past

She was sexually aggressive and just blew my mind

That should have been the first and last time

But

It was just like crack

I was instantly hooked

I saw my woman differently now

Every time that I looked at her

Compared to this new obsession

My heart and mind were no longer in my lady's possession

I didn't want to hurt her

But I had over abstained

And this new one kept me constantly drained

So now I'm the one controlled by that need

And I'll do anything

As long as she feeds

This hunger

In me

That won't seem to die

The thought of not having it makes me want to cry

I would give up anything as long as I can keep the feeling that she gives me that puts me to sleep

I gave up my woman

My kids might be next

I never thought that I would be addicted to sex

But I am

And I don't want rehabilitation

I don't see any way out of this situation

Probably wouldn't want it even if I could

Because the sex she gives me is just so good

A part of me says leave her alone and stay away

But I'm in too deep so I won't stop today

You can pray for me

If you think it might help

Because right now

I just can't help myself

Kiss and Tell

I called my baby and said

Dinner's ready

He said

What ya got

I told him I'd fix his plate when he got home but that wasn't the only thing that was hot

He said a hot plate and a hot woman you know that can't be beat

And you know yo' cookin' aint the only thing you got that I like to eat

I said I know baby and it's all waiting on you

The kids are gone for the weekend we can do what you want to

He said

If that's the case

You can put the plate on hold

'Cause I've got a hot woman that I don't want getting cold

I said you might want to eat your dinner first

Before you start on me

Because with the mood I'm in right now

You're going to need a LOT of energy

He said

Oh it's like that

Well then of course

Yes ma'am

I'll do whatever you say

Your wish is my command

I told him he might not want to say that until he knew what was on my mind

He said

Girl as much as you do for me

I can take orders this time

I said

First order of business

You have to clean your plate

You've been working all day and I plan on keeping you up late

Truth be told

I might not even let you sleep

We've been being quiet for the kids

Tonight

I want you to go deep

I want you to make me scream

Bite

Scratch

So you can remember why you said that

In love

You had met your match

He looked at me and said

My lady

As you wish

Dinner was good now it's time for my favorite dish

He pulled me close and his kisses began to rain all over me

My passion I could no longer contain

I wrapped my legs around him and felt him start to swell

As far as what happened next

Well

I don't kiss and tell

Round One

It's raining

I want to make love to you

But

You're not here so what can I do

I've been texting you

Letting you know my mood

I know that you're working

I'm trying to be good

I couldn't help but say what I did when you called home on your break

I want you more than a hungry lion wants some steak

Or

A thirsty man wants a tall glass of water

This rain

I want it to pass

Away from here

And let the sun come out

Because of all the things it's got me thinking about

Like

You coming home in clothes that are soaking wet

And

Me taking you into the bathroom and saying

Get out of those wet clothes so that you don't get sick

Then

Unzipping your pants saying

Let me show you a trick

I take off your shirt

Drop it on the floor

Turn on the shower

Check the lock on the door

The water may be hot but

You know that I'm hotter

I look at you and say

Why don't we work on that daughter that you want so much

It's a good time to start

I'm more than ready

If you'll do your part

We step into the shower

Our own private rain

And with the water hitting your back

You made me say your name

With my legs around your waist and my back against the wall

You were hitting it right and your name I began to call

Over and over

Like the chorus to my favorite song

You were giving it to me deep

Hard

And strong

You couldn't hold me up forever

And finally set me down

I thought that it was over t

Then you turned me around

You got it from the back with one hand on my hips

With the other reaching around and playing with my lips

The southern pair

I was biting the ones on top

Trying not to scream

Moaning

Baby please don't stop

And you didn't

You definitely passed that test

Then you took one hand and started playing with my breast

That spot on my neck

You began to lick and kiss

For me at that moment

That was the definition of sexual bliss

I was almost there my muscles began to squeeze

You stepped up your tempo and whispered

I aim to please

We were covered in sweat and the water was getting cold

My legs were getting weak and it took both of your hands to hold me up

Once I started shaking until the first waves had passed

As I wrapped the towel around me I said

That was the first round

But it definitely won't be the last

Nature

Copious amounts of moisture dripped from his tree

As he contemplated diving deep into her sea

She played the game and no desire was shown

As she thought of ways to soften his stone

Back and forth they went communicating with their eyes

The clouds above them increased as both their heat and moisture did rise

After a while all caution to the wind was thrown

And they entered the most natural yet private zone

Once he had finished swimming in her sea

Copious amounts of moisture dripped from his tree

Men or Frogs

You sextin' chicks

Exchangin' pics

But I'm not supposed to get mad

You wanna play

Yet continually say

That I'm the best you ever had

Sorry boo

That just won't do

You need to make a choice

Are you gonna stand

And be your own man

Or keep listenin' to your homie's voice

You know

The dude that says that it's ok to be a dog

Even though he's nothing more than a homeless 6 ft. frog

Hopping around from place to place

Never staying long

Can't keep a woman yet claims that his game is strong

Is that your hero

Is that how you want to be

If so

Please hop on past me

I'm not a little girl kissing frogs to find a prince

I'm the real woman that

When you're lonely

You're gonna miss

Make up your mind sweetie

I don't have all day

Are you a man or a frog

Let me know something either way

Quickie

I was standing in our bedroom with my robe on
Nothing on under it
Dancing to our song
You came up behind me
 Turned me around
Put an arm around my waist
And let the zipper down
Your hands slipped inside and caressed my skin
You looked at my breast and your eyes drank them in
My heart began to race as my body shook
I felt the heat from your hands and saw it in your look
I closed my eyes in anticipation of your kiss
But my lips
You deliberately missed
My nipples your mouth gently grasped
I showed my surprise with a moan and gasp
My legs began to shake so I stumbled to the bed
I wanted you to move up
But
You went down instead
The pleasure I was feeling suddenly intensified

I wrapped my legs around your head and took your tongue for a ride

And just when I thought that I couldn't take anymore

You pulled me to the edge of the bed and put my feet on the floor

Stood me up and put your chest against my back

Then you bent me over and gave my booty a smack

I was soaking wet so you slid right in

And that was when the real fun began

You were playing with my nipples and kissing on my neck

Orgasm after orgasm shook me

I couldn't keep my body in check

I guess that was ok 'cause we were short on time

You got yours and I definitely got mine

Until they came to the door I had forgotten about the kids

Even though it was quick

I'm glad you came when you did

Happy Birthday

No cake for you

But

Let me blow on your candle

I've got a special gift that I hope you can handle

That gift

Is me

No gift wrap required

I hope that you're ready

I hope you're not tired

See

I have to put it on you in a special way

Since that's all that I'm giving you for your birthday

First

I'll massage you

We've got all night

I think I'll wear that red and black nightie that you like

The one that doesn't cover much but somehow keeps me warm

Maybe it's just the heat from your gaze or the anticipation of being in your arms

Whatever it is

I have to keep it in check

I have a plan in mind that I don't want to wreck

Vanilla flavored massage oil that warms at a touch

Fruit

Wine

Candles

I hope that's not too much

I know that you're the man and this something that you would do

But

Since today is your birthday

Just let me cater to you

Let me turn the music on

Put the CD on repeat

You're going to need your energy

Go ahead and eat

Don't look at me like that

I meant the food

I'm glad to see that you're already in the mood to please me and to also be pleased

I hope you know that you're going to be teased

I'm going to touch and kiss

Suck and stroke

Take you in my mouth

I promise I won't choke

Now that dinner is over

Come and lay down

Let me massage your body

Rub my hands all around

Then follow my hands with my tongue to increase the heat

Your skin is salty but

The oil is sweet

I love the way you taste

The sounds that you make

Now it's time for the handcuffs so you can't escape

You smile as the locks snap into place

I just love that sexy look on your face

I get the oils and massage you again

You squirm beneath my touch while I just grin

I go slower this time without your hands to help

I know you'll pay me back

But I just can't help myself

So I let my fingers roam

I gladly take my time

Now it's time to lick the oil off

I want you to lose your mind

I know that you want the handcuffs to come off

But I'm too busy trying to make hard things soft

I made my way from your chest to even lower

And as your breathing got faster

My tongue got slower

I want to make sure that not one part do I skip

I'll play with your shaft while my tongue circles your tip

I can tell your ready to cum that first nut is so near

The sounds that give you away are music to my ears

My grip gets tighter and my pressure increases

I'm soaked from the sounds you made when you released

I take off the handcuffs and lay on your chest

And say

Baby

This is just the beginning of your birthday sex

Don't Bite Your Tongue

Don't bite your tongue say what you gotta say

If you don't want me then let me go today

Stop sneaking around doin' shit behind my back

Get with that chick if you think she got something I lack

You constantly doin' shit to piss on my trust

There's more to being a man than how many nuts you can bust

Chasin' behind anything with some tits and a split

Keep heading down that road and you know what you'll get

Something itchy that makes you feel like yo' dick's been stung

If you got something to say go ahead don't bite your tongue

You'd move to be with him you'd fuck him every night

You must be single with no kids and no job cuz that doesn't sound right

How you making all these promises to a nigga you aint neva met

Talkin' bout just lookin' at his pics makes you wet

Telling him that you are a pro at giving head
Aint no tellin' how many niggas done been in yo bed
Offerin' him yo' ass cuz I won't give him mine
Bitch is you crazy that shit is outta line
I know he got game and that smile got you sprung
You got something to say come on don't bite your tongue

But I really have no one to blame but myself
Thinking that you would change and need no one else
Thinking that these silly hoes would respect our relationship
They won't if you won't that's a little tip
A little advice from me to you
They only do what you allow them to
They wouldn't take this shit if they were me
Because you only show them what you want them to see
This is the last time that because of you my head is hung
You got anything else come on don't bite your tongue

Imagination

We've been fighting all day
And of course I'm mad at you
But now that we're alone
You react like you always do
You say
Take your anger out on me
I can handle it
I can take the scratches
I don't mind being bit
I look at you and tell you that the anger's still there but now there's something else
You better beware
You say
Your anger can wait 'til morning let's take a break
Although you may forget to be mad after the love we're about to make
After you've taken your frustrations out on my body I doubt you'll have the energy to still be mad at me
I could be wrong I guess we'll find out
Tonight
I plan on making you scream and shout
Not out of anger but

Pleasure instead

It's completely up to you if we ever reach the bed

Right here on the floor or up against the wall

Whatever you can think of

We can do it all

My response was

I'll still be mad tomorrow when I wake up

If you think good sex will fix it

Then you are out of luck

But

To turn you down I would have to be a fool

And since don't go to bed mad is our number one rule we shouldn't go to bed at all 'cause I'm still hot

You think you can calm me down

Come on

Show me what you got

Can you make me forget why I was mad in the first place

Why a part of me still wants to slap your face

If you can

Feel free

This is my kind of fight

I can easily hold you down and

Yes

I will scratch and bite

I know my anger excites you

That comes as no surprise

You can't hide your reaction

I can see it in your eyes

And

There are other things that make it perfectly clear

I have someplace for that so bring it over here

We can take a break from the verbal sparring for a private wrestling match

Tomorrow

When you're at work you'll feel every bite and scratch

Then maybe you'll regret making me this mad

Or

Maybe you'll think it was the best you ever had

Your response was silence you simply stood and stared

The challenge had been issued for me to accept if I dared

Which I did

What would you have done in that situation

And as far as what happened next

Well

I'll leave that to your imagination

Round Two

We went to the bedroom to have more room to dry
You took the towel
Then placed a hand on my thigh
I stood there shaking
But I wasn't cold
It was the look in your eyes as you watched the water roll down my body and onto the floor
I could tell from that look that you wanted more
And so did I
The rain was still falling
Even a deaf man could hear my body calling
And a blind woman could see your desire
I was more than ready to feel the fire
You pulled me close and kissed me nice and slow
I tried to hold back a moan but I had to let it go
Your body responded to the sounds that I made
I was quickly picked up
On the bed I was laid
The heat between us burned away all my words
Yet each of my desires you obviously heard
You moved slowly and your body became my cover

You have always been a most thorough and attentive lover

Tonight was no exception

You read my body well

I reached down to stroke you as you once again began to swell

You pulled back to let my hands be free

And I guided you to where you most wanted to be

Every time feels like the first time you softly said

As I was squeezing you and arching up off the bed

I nibbled your ear and then your neck

I was in a hurry but you kept me in check

You set the tempo at a very slow pace

I know you enjoyed the looks on my face

I think I was still sensitive from our time in the shower

Because it felt like your strokes had so much power

Maybe it was the fact that you were being such a tease

All I know is my legs were shaking and I couldn't feel my knees

I knew that they were there because my feet were flat

I must've been bad the way you were beating this cat

Or maybe it was good

I really can't say

I just knew that you were draining me and I couldn't stay that way
Either you read my mind or our issues were the same
Because you suddenly changed tempo and quickly we came
You rolled onto your back and pulled me to your side
Said baby
I haven't forgotten how much you like to ride
But I've been working all day and I need some food
Please fix me a plate then I'll lay back and be good
I got up
Put on my robe and said
I like the way that sounds
And you do need your energy because I want a few more rounds

Thanks

You traded shit for sugar but
That's fine with me
I love having access to that fiyah head and sweet pussy
You called it your Puddin is what she said
I call it a meal because she keeps me well fed
You couldn't handle her so you made her feel less
Even though she was real and gave you her best
Breakfast
Dinner
Sometimes lunch or a snack
Soon as I leave her
I want to go back for just a little more of what you threw away
Man
I'm gone shake your hand if we meet one day
Because what you treated like trash is my most precious treasure
She gives me all types of sexual pleasures
And takes care of me in every way a woman should
Not just with sex
Her cooking and conversation is better than good

She is the type of woman that makes me glad that I waited

Her mind is amazing

You were just intimidated

Again I thank you

I plan on giving her my last name

While you keep trying to be a player and playing high school games

Your mind didn't intrigue her

Your dick couldn't satisfy

So you did your best to hurt her and make her cry

But she survived it and you can't seem to understand why you see her smiling again

It's 'cause she's with a real man

Now you regret your decision and want this queen back

But it's too late because I showed her all the things that you lacked

I put it on her whenever she wants me to

I've made her smile and forget all about you

So go ahead and keep chasing those peasants with low self-esteem

You can't call yourself a king because you passed on having a queen

At the Altar

When he comes to worship
He kneels before my throne
He is my king
And with me
He is home
He speaks a special language as he kneels between my knees that awakens something deep inside that he just loves to see
He takes his time
Chanting slowly to my pearl
Causing feelings and reactions that make my head swirl
The sounds from the altar are meant for only us to hear
Although we don't care if others may be near
There's no need for instructions
He worships very well
There's no need for improvement
As far as I can tell
When he speaks in tongues
Heaven is below my waist
He always says he loves how his Karmel angel tastes
Of course
I bow at his altar as often as he does mine

Sometimes I'm the six

Other times the nine

I love to stroke and kiss his scepter

Because when he is well-pleased

It releases the sweetest nectar

He bows before his queen whenever he gets the chance

And I love kissing my king's ring it increases the romance

When it's time to release and set love free

At the altar is where I long to be

After Dinner Surprise

Sit back and relax baby you've had a long day
I'm going to make you feel better in a special way
Let me take off your shoes and massage your feet
Then I'll bring you your dinner so that you can eat
After you're done with dinner just stay in your chair
I'm going to shower you with tender loving care
Let me unbutton your shirt and loosen your belt
A part of you wants to break free so let me help
I know he feels better now that he's free
He's standing at attention and that one eye is looking at me
To the top of his head I apply a gentle kiss
And hold him softly while I'm doing this
You lean your head back and close your eyes
While I continue with my after dinner surprise
You're my favorite flavor just in case you didn't know
Which is why I'm taking my time and kissing him nice and slow
You're pulling my hair while you growl and moan
That excites me so much that I just have to jump on
I stand up and open my robe
Straddle you and place my Karmel globes

Right in your face so you have no choice

But to suck on them and take me to soaked from moist

My riding rhythm matches the rhythm of your tongue

And I quickly lose count of the times that I cum

No matter the number I'll always take more

You get tired of the chair so we move to the floor

Now that we have more room I get down on my hands and knees

I know that you like it like that and I aim to please

While you're playing with my nipples and kissing on my neck

I don't even try to keep my moans in check

I'm throwing it back at you and taking every stroke

You givin' it to me good yo lovin' aint no joke

My legs have gotten weak I've cum so many times

This was supposed to be about you but you made sure that I got mine

Over and over more times than I could count

You showed me once again what good lovin' is about

Your growls start getting deeper as you speed up your pace

And as you cum inside me we collapse in place

Too tired to move we lay there with matching grins

Knowing that once we catch our breath we're doing it all again

More Than a Freak

He told you all the things that his woman didn't know
You used that knowledge to help him let go
Of their relationship
And all they had built
You played to his libido
Manipulated his guilt
Now he's cheating on you and you want to act confused
Upset that another woman knows the same tactics that *you* used
What goes around comes around
Right back to you
You've finally learned that the old saying is true
It's not just something that the old folks say
You WILL get what you give
Somehow
Some way
Do you remember that woman and how you laughed
You didn't care about her tears as long as you had him
He was your prize
Your number one goal
You could've cared less about the one he left out in the cold

But now that woman is you and you can't seem to understand

Why your actions couldn't change that man

You gave him everything he wanted

Did everything he said

Was his freak anytime he asked

In and out of bed

You let him do what he wanted

Swallowed more than just your pride

Now you're trying to figure out why you've been pushed aside

It's actually quite simple

You were just a toy that is no longer any fun to that selfish little boy

Disguised as a man

Who likes playing heart games

Hopefully you learned your lesson or else there'll be more of the same

Situations

For you

Later on in life

Because a man wants more than a freak when he's ready for a wife

Tonight

Let me fuck you baby

Yeah

You heard me right

I know I don't usually talk like this

But I am *extremely* horny tonight

I want to start by

Letting your head touch the back of my throat

Then acting out **all** of the fantasies that I wrote

When I let my

Karmel side cum out to play

And when I'm done

All I want you to say is

Damn baby

That was good

The best I ever had

You are definitely the best

When you choose to be bad

But

That's only if you have the energy to speak

Because I plan on draining you and making you weak

I want to suck you dry and make you say my name

Then I want to ride you

You're one horse I plan to tame

But I don't want your dick to have all the fun

Before the night is over

You're gonna have to use your tongue

Sixty-nine isn't my favorite position but it sure is nice

Then I want to use the blindfolds

The handcuffs

Maybe even some ice

The good girl in me was tired so she went to sleep

The bad girl wants her legs on your shoulders so you can go deep

All in balls out

That's what I want from you

I want to be curled up sleeping like a baby once you're through

From the bed to the floor then up against the wall

I want it in the shower

Hell I'll even take it in the hall

You're going to be tired tomorrow but you won't mind

You'll spend most of the day at work thinking about our time

It's a good thing our neighbors don't live too near

They'd be surprised and maybe a little excited by the sounds that they'd hear

All the screams and moans that show our pleasure

From me licking your pole and your tongue finding my treasure

You're going to have to hit it hard deep and right

Because the good girl is sleep and

Baby

I need you to fuck me tonight

Your Wife

We were standing there talking
But you couldn't hear me
The desire in my eyes
You were too distracted to see
So when you turned and walked away I had to give chase
I didn't even let you turn around
Just kissed your back on that special place
That let you know exactly what was on my mind
But you turned and said
Baby
I don't have time
I bit my lip and said baby please
Rubbed the front of your pants
Gave a gentle squeeze
Kissed you lightly
And nibbled on your lip
You said
I guess my morning meeting could be skipped
I said
Just a quickie baby
I promise that's all
As I unzipped your pants your job got a call
The shirt came off
The pants hit the floor
The kids were asleep but I still locked the door
You took control

You knew just what to do
And made me glad
Once again
That I had married you
I tried my best to not get too loud
But you were doing things that would make a porn star proud
Your strokes were strong
I couldn't help but shake
You were giving me as much as I could take
Rubbing and touching
Your hands were like fire
And your mouth
Mmmmmmmm
It just increased my desire
I wrapped my legs around you and held on for dear life
And when it was over
I was so glad that I was your wife

Round Three

I got up to fix you dinner but
You wanted to help
I couldn't focus with your hands under my robe so I said
Do it yourself
You took over in the kitchen just like you do in the bedroom
My knees got weak watching your tongue work around that spoon
You bring home the bacon
And cook it up too
And in the bedroom
You make sure I don't need anyone but you
When dinner was over
You said let me rub you down
I know you're tense from having the kids inside all day running around
You've taken care of me but now it's my turn
I want to use my hands to put your body on a slow burn
I want to get you so hot that you pin me to the bed
Since we don't have a horse you can ride me instead
I won't throw you off although I might buck
You'll have to lean down so on your nipples I can suck
I laid on the bed and turned my back to you
And said stop talking and do what you're going to
Your hands did wonders to rekindle my fires
All that massage did was strengthen my desire

It did finally get to a point where I had to attack
And as usual
You let me win our private wrestling match
You were at full attention
The perfect soldier
Seeing your body's reaction to me just made me bolder
So my hands went to work making your temperature rise
I knew I was rubbing you right when you closed your eyes
Your hands started rubbing me and you started to squirm and moan
I leaned in to kiss you
Your mouth looked so alone
That kiss must've done it because you said baby please
So I sat up and rocked back on my knees
I took my hand and guided you inside
Then I took my favorite horse for a ride
The tempo changed so many times that I lost count
I pulled you up to kiss you to muffle both our shouts
From soft and slow to hard and fast
With my legs wrapped around you
I didn't think that I could last
Then you moved my legs so that you could lie back down
Your hands were on my stomach
Back
Breasts
Just all around

Then you pulled me closer and took my breasts in your mouth

What your mouth did in the north caused explosions in the south

My explosions were like a match to your fuse

I knew you were close

Your body gave me clues

First you started to growl

Then your muscles got tight

I still wasn't tired of hearing you

Even if it was the third time that night

As you sat up I laid back on your legs with my head by your feet

I wrapped my legs around you again and the feeling was real sweet

I felt you explode inside me as you made that growling sound

And as you collapsed onto the bed I thought

Now *that* was one hell of a round

Show Me

The year of the dragon is when I made my debut
In the month of February
Day number two
That makes me an Aquarius
In case you couldn't tell
And I promise this water baby can make your head swell
Until it's harder than Chinese math etched in stone
Then I'll take the time to make you gasp and moan
See
I'm all about exploring and learning new things
Like how to make your dick jump or your body sing
Teach me how to please you
I like to learn
Just know that my moans
You will have to earn
No faking here
That's a waste of energy
I'm cold enough to tell you if you're not pleasing me
I guess it's just that water in my veins
But don't worry
I'll still make you say my name
I'll have you sweating
Needing a break
Wondering how much more you can take
While I'm just chilling
Cool as ice

If you think you can handle me
You better think twice
I admit that I haven't had fun with every sign
But there are a couple that make me constantly get mine
Them lions be having me purring in pleasure
Giving me that good stuff after finding my treasure
And those Libras be tipping scales and more
Having me sending pics of me on all fours
Or something even freakier than that
Anything to have him throwing me on my back
So he can beat it up like a real man should
While whispering in my ear telling me it's good
Trying to see how deep he can get
Keeping this Aquarian nice and wet
By getting his face wet telling me I taste sweet
Steadily switching positions and messing up sheets
So I figure the best sex signs number only three
If you think I'm wrong
Then I guess you'll just have to show me

The Stroll

He was in no hurry
This was just an evening stroll
He took his time so as to ensure that I would lose control
His hands were his eyes on this exceptional night
And he took the scenic route
Taking in all the sights
He began his journey by tracing the outskirts
Creating anticipation so intense that it almost hurt
After removing the speed bumps created by my gown
He slowly made his way to the center of town
His tongue now joined his fingers in his exploration
Making sure that I experienced some very pleasant sensations
He made it to the hills and began to explore
Doing things that had me whimpering and begging for more
Obviously the directions I was giving were being misread
Because I wanted him to cum north but he went south instead
He slowly traversed the pool in the middle of the woods
Taking his time like a real explorer should
Making sure to find every treasure
Every secret spot
And not backing down when things got a little hot
After causing tremors and vibrations to radiate from my center
He found what he was looking for and began to slowly enter
Ever the explorer
He continued to take it slow
Because all the ways to please me
He wanted to know

Even when I wanted to pick up the pace and was out of control
He stayed calm because
For him
This wasn't a race
Just a leisurely stroll

New Toy

Well
My bullet is broke
The pocket rocket is a joke
That I'm tired of laughing at
Need a big dog to cum handle this cat
No more plastic or battery operated
I need a man who has graduated
Magna cum lawdy
With a PHD
That's a Pleasing Her Degree
See my orgasm is trapped
I can't seem to set it free
Somebody needs to help me
It's gonna take some work
This is gonna take more than a bachelor
Gotta be a master
At causing natural disasters
And making the tide rise
Between my thighs
I have a high sex drive
A rookie won't survive
Handling these curves
Takes a lotta nerve
Can you put the hammer down
Have me holding on
As you work it around
Or are you just another toy for me trash
Unable to really get in this ass
The way I need you to
You might wanna grow an inch or two

And take some ginseng
Improve your endurance
Make sure you've got some good insurance
See
I need a Cupid who can shoot all night
I can be your quiver
Your bow will fit just right
But
If that perfect paramour is not you
Then another vibrator will just have to do

Breaking Point

Every woman has a breaking point
In case you didn't know
A point which
Past it
She simply cannot go
It's different for every woman and every case
You'll know when she's reached it by the lack of tears on her face
There'll be no more crying
No more screams
Her nightmares have already been replaced by sweet dreams
Dreams of a man who knows her worth
Who will cherish her above any woman on earth
She's accepted that the man of her dreams is not you
And that your relationship has long ago been through
She's just going through the motions for whatever reason
But your time in her life is up
It's the end of your season
Just be grateful that she doesn't have violent tendencies

She could've busted your car's windows or scratched it with her keys
Or been waiting when you came home on one of those late nights with a bat or a gun
I'd advise you to be careful before you mistreat the next one
She may not be as patient and her fuse may blow quick
You'll go to sleep whole and wake up missing your dick
Or
You could be the straw that breaks the camel's back
And she could follow you to your side piece then start the attack
Don't take for granted that she's going to keep taking that emotional abuse
Be prepared for her to wake up one day and realize that
For you
She has no use
You may one day come home to an empty house
Or eat a meal laced with poison meant for a mouse
Which is what you acted like when she was away
Finding anyone willing to let you cum and play
So take heed to this warning
It can save time

Money

And maybe your life

Don't think that you can keep mistreating your girlfriend or wife

If you do

Don't be surprised to one day find a zero balance in the account that was joint

Because every woman on this planet has their own specific breaking point

Inhibitions

Inhibitions
Yeah I've got a few
But that won't stop me from pleasing you
At fellatio 101
I graduated head of the class
But I refuse to let you put it in my ass
I don't mind if it gets a little rough
But I don't do whips
Chains
Or handcuffs
I will do what I can to set your seed free
As long as it's understood that it's just you and me
There'll be no extra parties
This is a private affair
One or the other because I refuse to share
You'll forget about my no's when I make you say yes
I just had to get those things off my chest

The Story of We

Stuttering from the force of my pen on his pad
Exclaiming these words were the best he'd ever had
He lets me write a story worthy of the best sellers list
It begins and ends with a simple kiss
Well maybe not that simple
Let me explain
This kiss was brought on by the sound of the rain
The rhythm that was being played on the skylight
Was guaranteed to keep us up all night
Not because it was so loud
Don't get me wrong
It was because the rain has always been our favorite song
Sometimes we match the rhythm
Sometimes we change the beat
He does things to make me wetter than a flooded street
And I return the favor making him harder than petrified wood
See
The rain washes away our inhibitions so it's hard to be good
No need to behave or worry about the sounds
We get lost in each other with no desire to be found
His kisses fall on me steadily matching the rainfall
Causing my downpour as god's name I call
As the thunder crashes
Our bodies collide
Together we create our own storm inside
He causes floods
I soak his tree
I love it when he lets me write the story of we

Round Four

I crawled up to your chest and listened to your heartbeat slow
Trying to figure out how many more rounds my body would be willing to go
I thought I had one more in me
Maybe two
But I wasn't so sure about you
You had been working all day and now into the night
My taking all of your energy just didn't seem right
But you pulled me on top of you and kissed me slow and deep
Letting me know that there wasn't one drop of energy that you wanted to keep
The rain was still falling outside so I was still game to let you do whatever you wanted to do to make me say your name
You flipped us over and the kisses got deeper
I was reminded of one of the many reasons that I knew you were a keeper
From my mouth you moved down to kiss me on my neck
And when you moved lower
It was hard to keep my moans in check
I squirmed beneath you
My hands rubbing your back and head
Wanting you to stay where you were but feeling you going lower instead

I had to bite the pillow when you swirled my belly button with your tongue

And when you found my pearl I almost came undone

Part of me wanted to run while the other part wanted to hold you down

And while I was torn your tongue continued moving all around

Fast

Slow

Up

Down

In and out

The things that you were doing had me wanting to shout

You held me down when I tried to run away

And after that there was nothing left for me to say

You slid in while I was still shaking and trying to catch my breath

After what you had just done I didn't think that I had any energy left

But

That first stroke obviously hit the right spot

Because I was back in the game giving it all I've got

I wrapped my arms around your neck and my legs around your waist

You were taking me for a ride and I wasn't letting you go any place

You kept changing the tempo like a DJ that was high

I kept up despite the tremors in my thighs

I knew you had to go to work in the morning but I really didn't care

Especially when you rocked back on your knees and put my legs up in the air

And when you started slow stroking with the intent to tease

You did something that made me lose the feeling in my knees

I should've been drained

There should've been no more

But when you stood up and put my feet on the floor

I was energized by the thought of the new levels of pleasure my body would soon meet

And as you got it from the back I screamed into the sheets

With one hand in my hair and the other on my breast

You kissed the back of my neck and I no longer wanted rest

I said

One more time against the wall before this is over

But you couldn't hear me

My face was still in the cover

So I found the strength to push off of the bed and stand

To make sure that you could hear my command

You turned me around and put me up against the wall

And I held on for dear life as you gave me your all

Explosion after explosion made my body shake

I wasn't sure how much more I could take

After a while your legs got weak

So a new position you chose to seek

But walking was something that neither one of us could do

So you laid back onto the floor and pulled me on top of you

You were almost there so I didn't have to do much work

You squeezed my thighs as I felt your body spasm and jerk

I fell on your chest because I was more than done

And thought to myself

That had to be the last one

Regale Me

He said
"Regale me
Tell me
A bedtime story"
So
I went back in my mind
And told him about the time
That he had put me to bed
Loving me thoroughly
From feet
To head
And not missing one point in between
Making the walls blush from our love scene
It started with a look in his eyes
Then the kiss
His hands on my thighs
Immediately I kissed him back
He is my favorite aphrodisiac
Hands explored as his tongue paved the way
No need to speak
He heard what my body had to say
Soaked the sheets from our foreplay
His tongue knew the combination
His hands opened the door
He had me stuttering and stammering trying to ask for more
No need for me to speak
He knew how to make me weak
Tasting both sets of lips
Taking more than just sips
Dipping deep into my well

Leaving me under his spell
He was my horse
I was his bitch
Never knew when he would switch
Had me playing a guessing game
Felt so good
I forgot my name
His name also escaped my mind
Caused spasms of the multiple kind
Like a champ he rode my waves
Explored the interior of my caves
Found the treasure that he sought
Won all the rounds that we fought
Gave me the kind of pleasure that made me weep
A harvest of orgasms he gladly reaped
But
My story didn't put him to sleep
Reminded him of all our fun
So after the story ended
Our night begun

Next Best Thing

I woke up early
Feeling some type of way
I called my man not knowing what I was going to say
But when he answered
And I heard his sleepy voice
The thoughts that came to mind had me instantly moist
I moaned
Good morning I was just thinking about you
Wishing you were here so that we could do
Some things
Start this day off right
Make me glow and make your steps light
He laughed that sleepy laugh that I love
And said
That's what I was just thinking of
Then he reminded me that he always wakes up hard
And I realized that across town was just too far
For me to drive
Before we both had to be to work
But his words were making me so horny that it hurt
Telling me that he was playing with his bone
Pretending it was me then he started to moan
That made me moan and squirm in the bed
Wishing my hands were his instead
Although it felt so good I really didn't care
Because his words and moans were definitely taking me there
He kept telling me what he wanted to do and I responded in kind
His voice was so sexy it was messing with my mind

When his breathing got heavy I knew he was close
Which was fine by me
'cause my hands were soaked
I listened to him growl and call my name
When the line went quiet I knew that he'd came
After a minute I said
Baby are you okay
He said yep
That was a good way to start the day
I laughed and said I'm glad you picked up when you heard the phone ring
Because
Since you couldn't be here
This was the next best thing

A Hard Day

We were lying together at the end of a long day
You were tired
But
I was feeling a certain way
I tried to behave
I didn't want to press
But the sound of your voice and the soft caress
Of your hand
As you stroked my back
Woke that beast within and made her attack
I tried to restrain her because I didn't want to move
So I let my hands roam over you
Your skin was so smooth
But that wasn't enough
My mouth wanted in on the fun
So I kissed your chest
But I couldn't stop at just one
As my kisses increased
Your words got slower
Then my mouth decided to go lower
You stopped me and said
Baby I'm tired
I said
Baby I got this
I'm feeling inspired
When I started down again
You didn't try to make me stop

You just laid there and let me use you like a blow pop

I just wanted to help you sleep

That was my only goal

But you were rejuvenated and suddenly took control

Somehow we went from lying down to sitting on the edge of the bed

My back was against your chest and I was looking straight ahead

Although I wasn't seeing much

My eyes were partially closed

The things you were doing had me moaning and curling my toes

Your mouth on the back of my neck

Hands trailing between my breasts and thighs

Through making me weak you became energized

Because suddenly we were standing and I was looking at the floor

I realized that was supposed to be quick would probably leave me sore

You had one hand on my hip the other in my hair

My legs were getting weak

I needed to lean on the chair

But you knew my body

You read it like a book

You picked me up and laid me on my back as my legs shook

I knew that you were tired and figured that our loving was at an end

Then you gave me a look that let me know that it was just about to begin

You used your tongue to work the soreness out

Showed me all the things that you could do with your mouth

Your hands massaged my nipples as your tongue massaged something else

I squirmed and screamed

I just couldn't control myself

Finally you came up and your mouth replaced your hands

I begged for you to fill me but you ignored my demands

You didn't want me to just be wet

You wanted me soaked

I tried to show you that my fires had been properly stoked

You listened to me begging for a few minutes longer

I know you enjoyed it

It made your desire stronger

I was impatient

But you set the pace

You entered slowly

Watching my face

Around your waist is where my legs were quickly wrapped

I didn't want to let you go

I thought I had you trapped

You must've liked it you didn't tell me to let go

In fact your strokes got stronger

Nice and slow

My reactions to your loving just made you bolder

Because you grabbed my legs and put them on your shoulders

Your mouth went back to work it must've been on break

Putting my thighs close to your mouth was a definite mistake

Then you started slow strokin' taking him in and out

Your mouth left my thighs and made its way to my mouth

You must've thought I was tired because you gave my mouth a rest

And worked your way down to my neck and then my breast

My body was affecting you and you knew you wouldn't last

So you strengthened your strokes and started hitting fast

Sucking on my toes while you were deep strokin'

Was the perfect way to create an explosion

We came together and breathless in each other's arms we lay

And all this started because you were telling that you'd had a hard day

Magnify

Let me get my magnifying glass
Boy please
How you gone regulate this ass
With that little thing
Here's your hall pass
You need to get back to class
Before the bell rings
Make sure you pay attention
When the teacher starts to mention
How to use your tongue
Or else face suspension
Because when your soldier's at attention
He doesn't impress anyone
Your game is as strong as a light fog
Did you really compare that twig to a log
Let me get my magnifying glass
You couldn't bring the sausage if you bought a whole hog
I've seen bigger wieners in a hot dog
Boy please
How you gone regulate this ass

Neighbors

I see him watching me whenever I go outside
I knew if I asked him he'd let me take a ride
On him as if he were the seats of my car
But I didn't know if we'd ever get that far
See all he's ever done is waved and smiled
He looks sweet and innocent but he may be wild
He may be into whips and chains and all kinds of stuff
And may hear something completely different when I say I like it rough
His body's nice and his eyes are so kind
I just wish I knew what was going on in his mind

She's so beautiful I can't help but stare
I have to wonder if she's even aware
Of the effect that her body has on mine
Or the thoughts that her smile puts in my mind
I wonder if she'd smile like that with her legs in the air
If she'd let me spank her and pull her hair
She's probably not even into that kind of stuff
She'd probably get scared if I got a little rough
I can't walk away from my car and that's a shame
She can make my body jump and I don't even know her name

The waiting for him to act was making me weak

So the next time I saw him I decided to speak

The look in his eyes told me everything

I could see that he wanted to try to make my body sing

My heartbeat increased while my body started to throb

I wondered how long the interview would last before I gave him the job

We talked for a while and I learned his name

I still couldn't tell if he was wild or tame

My eyes drank him in as I let my mind roam

I couldn't wait to get to work so I could hurry back home

I watched her walk to her car when the conversation ended

And I must admit that the view was splendid

I replayed our little tête-à-tête in my mind

And hoped that she would one day be mine

I wondered if she was flirting or that was just my imagination

If she wanted me she could have me with no hesitation

She had a way about her

Her very own style

And I had been dreaming of her for quite a while

I just didn't know how to make that known

She makes me feel like a teenager even though I'm grown

Our first conversation has led to our first date

I'm so excited that I just can't wait
He won't tell me what he has planned
But I know what I'd love to do with that man
Not just the physical but emotional as well
How far he wants to go I really can't tell
I guess that I'll find out tonight
I hope that everything I say is right
Because I am as nervous as a little girl
Trying to figure out how to keep him in my world

Tonight's the night no more talking across cars
No more pretending I'm not watching her work in the yard
I'm not sure how this night will end
I just know I'm ready for it to begin
When she said yes I chose a restaurant quick
So I hope she likes the one that I picked
I don't want her to feel like she owes me a thing
I just want to see her smile and make her heart sing
It's finally time so I walked to her door
It takes everything in me to keep my jaw off the floor

    I was so nervous when I went to the door that my hands shook
    But my confidence returned when I saw his look
    The night kept getting better from the moment he offered me his arm

He was ever the gentleman after he turned on the charm
The meal was superb the company even better
The wine and the conversation had me getting wetter
I wanted him so badly that I didn't want to wait
But I knew a lady wasn't supposed to give it up on the first date
All the way home I wondered and worried about this
Hoping that when he dropped me off I'd at least get a kiss

When I walked her to the door I just couldn't help myself
So I asked her if there was anyone else
Her answer caused my heart to skip a beat
So I hugged her close lifting her off of her feet
When I put her down she bumped my thighs
And I stood there staring into her eyes
Hoping that as long as we had that connection
She wouldn't pay attention to my erection
But she stepped closer invading my space
Reached up and put her hand on my face

I had tried to fight it but the feeling was so strong
After he hugged me I knew I couldn't be wrong
When I moved closer I knew he wanted me too
And it was just natural to make one from the two
I kissed him then led him into my home

From the entrance to the bedroom he allowed my hands to roam
    He let me undress him one button at a time
    Assuring me that he had long wanted to be mine
    Once our clothes were in piles on the floor
    He finally pulled me close and began to explore

    The taste of her skin was a nectar so sweet
    Her moans made me shiver despite our combined heat
    I wanted to be tender but she scratched out an ancient song
    That made the monster in me want to give it to her hard and strong
    She didn't seem to mind from the reaction that I got
    Any thought of this being a one-time thing was shot
    As I stroked her deeper she chanted my name
    And I knew that my life would never be the same
    The next morning when we were finally through
    She looked at me with a smile and said can I keep you

Round Five

 I kissed you lightly on the lips and started crawling towards the bed
 And that vision must have sent the blood *straight* to your head
 Not the one with ears
 That smiles and has teeth
 But the one that had spent most of the night buried in my moist sheath
 You waited until I had pulled myself up on my knees
 Then reached over and gave my butt a gentle squeeze
 You crawled up behind me and whispered in my ear so soft
 We can go one more round
 Tomorrow is my day off
 As I climbed onto the bed you trailed kisses down my back
 That was enough to give me the energy that I lacked
 I laid back on the pillows and opened wide
 You climbed on top and slipped inside
 This wasn't about release but simple pleasure
 Given to the one that you loved beyond measure
 The tempo was slow and the kisses were deep
 I knew when this one was over we were both going to sleep
 There was no need to switch positions and the rhythm stayed steady

I tried hard to hold back until I knew that you were ready

I had lost count of the times you had pushed me over the edge that night

But I just couldn't fight it because your strokes were just right

You were right there with me my spasms started yours

And when you were done I knew there would be no more

At least not tonight

Sleep was insistently calling

And as I answered the Sandman

I could still hear the rain falling

Stop Frontin'

You rubbin' yo' dick
As you look at her pic
But around ya boys you complain

You say she'll never be a wife
While livin' that life
Then be on the front row makin' it rain

Hypocritical negro go sit down
And stop trying to clown
If you don't like it you don't have to look
Nobody's forcing you to be on Facebook
You wouldn't see half those pics if you hadn't like that page
But you realized you couldn't have them so you flew into a rage
It made me laugh when you said what you did
Claiming to be a man but acting like a kid
You threw a tantrum like a two-year old in a toy store
'Cause you wanted to see new pics but she wasn't posting anymore
Then you tried front and act all pious and chaste
Even though you jack off to thoughts of that slim waist

Her pics pop into your mind
At the oddest of times
Causing you stress and strife

But while you're focused on her
Has it never occurred
That you've been alone most of your life

There's no need to wonder
Why you can't get any numbers
You imagine her face on other chicks

So stop frontin' boy
You know you get joy
From lookin' at her pics

Heat

The numbers on the thermostat read a hundred and three
But that was nothing compared to the heat between you and me
There was an inferno raging
An all-consuming fire
The walls shook from the strength of our desire
Or maybe it was the headboard making them shake
We were causing our own personal earthquake
There were tremors created by the bounce of the mattress's springs
Just thinking about your skills in the bed makes my body sing
But you weren't doing all the work on your own
I was doing my point to make you grunt and moan
My hands and my hips were in constant motion
I kept your wood immersed in the depth of my ocean
As we maneuvered from one place to another
You proved to be a strong and flexible lover
Positions I'd never tried caused pleasure unparalleled
When I thought that it was over you once again swelled
I admit I was tired and just a little sore
But not so much that I couldn't give you more
There was more heavy breathing
More drops of sweat
And the use of positions that we hadn't tried yet
Incoherent mumblings
Sighs moans and screams
You did things to me I had never dreamed
And I returned the favor
Making sure that it was good

Because you were putting in work just like a man should
And I was content to be your project of choice
By the time the sun came up I had lost my voice
But it was worth it
I had finally put you to sleep
With the type of loving that can make a man weep
Because it was better than anything you ever had running those streets
As we lay satisfied in each other's arms we couldn't even feel the heat

The Recipe

I woke up to a pitched tent
In the middle of my bed
That pole was heaven sent
Remove the canvas
Now it's exposed
I am so glad that he doesn't sleep in clothes
No need for an alarm clock when you have me
I woke him up
The same way I put him to sleep
Pay attention
Here's the recipe
Slow circles from a warm tongue
Are the quickest way to make him cum
When added to gentle suction at the right amount
That's almost enough to knock him out
Include a hand with the perfect grip
While the mouth continues to sip
Throw in some Pop Rocks and a little humming
Then he'll have a hard time not cumming
This is the perfect equation
To create the exact sensation
Needed to make
An early morning protein shake

Forbidden Pleasure

I know I shouldn't be doing this
I know that it's wrong
I've tried to resist it
But the feeling is just too strong
I should've stopped myself when it was just a thought
But then our eyes met and I knew I was caught
In his eyes I saw reflections of my own hunger and desire
I stopped caring about everything else
I had to feel his fire
My husband had stopped looking at me like that a long time ago
At some point I had become his trophy wife
I was only for show
Now here was a man whose body called out to the woman in me
Whose looks made me dream about things that I knew shouldn't be
I tried to think of my husband when I looked at this man
I even tried to think of his wife when I saw his wedding band
But it didn't work
That desire was awake and I couldn't put it back to sleep
I kept having visions of gripping his back while he was going in deep

I couldn't stop myself from fantasizing
Those thoughts kept me moist
I knew that there was no turning back the first time I heard his voice
He spoke to me and suddenly my knees went weak
Ways to hear his bedroom voice I really wanted to seek
I fought the urge at first and I think that he did too
I talked to my husband and told him what I needed him to do
But just like in times past
My pleas fell on deaf ears
He had gotten complacent
We had been comfortable together for too many years
I could tell this man was having the same issues in his life
Because there's no way he'd be looking at me like that if he was satisfied with his wife
It started out so simple
Just smiling as we passed in the hall
Now we're in this room both hoping that our spouses don't call
At least that's what I was thinking when I first saw the bed
Then he kissed me and all thoughts flew from my head
Being in his arms with his mouth on mine
Made me feel more alive than I had in a long time
Our clothes disappeared
Our hands needed room to roam

His mouth and hands gave me feelings that I had never known

Or at least that I couldn't recollect

I stopped trying to keep myself in check

We ended up on the bed

I can't even remember how

I know that I should feel guilty but I didn't then and I don't now

Someone was finally taking the time to uncover my hidden treasure

And I enjoyed every minute of our forbidden pleasure

Knocked Out

He thought that he had beat me
He thought that I was done
But I'm like a pro fighter and that was just round one
He was definitely good
I had to admit that
But him and his big boy couldn't handle this cat
Yes I was winded but I still wanted more
There were so many positions yet to explore
I got up and followed him to the next room
And told him that it would be time to start again soon
He looked shocked and I just smiled
Then gave him a look to show that things were going to get wild
I went back to the room and lit the candles that he had ignored
When he came back I was in the middle of the bed on all fours
He came in and knew just what to do
This was the beginning of our round two
He hit it from the back and I enjoyed every stroke
I was throwin' it back at him like I was goin' for broke
He said slow down girl and gave my butt a smack
I said I'm just getting started
This isn't a snack
I'm a gourmet meal and you will be thoroughly satisfied

When you're tired of this position I'm ready for another ride
I don't know if it was my words or my actions
But I felt him start to shake
After he came he whispered I don't know how much more I can take
He fell onto the bed and onto his back he did roll
I looked at him and said
Don't worry I'll take control
I reached down and stroked him said big boy looks tired
But don't worry I have ways of stoking that fire
I got up left the room and brought back a warm towel
Cleaned him up and said
Now I'm going to make you growl
I'm going to do things to you to bring out the beast
I love sausage and you've brought me a feast
I climbed on top and gave him a kiss
Started stroking big boy and he started to hiss
I moved down to his neck while increasing the pressure with my hand
When I moved down to his chest I knew he was under my command
I hadn't made him growl yet just breath hard and moan
But my mouth had yet to make it to his growling zone
His breath got shallower as my head moved further south
You should have heard him when my hand was replaced by my mouth

I wish I could tell you what he said but they weren't exactly words

But I could tell that he was pleased by the sounds that I heard

I didn't want him to cum yet I figured one more was all that he had

And when I got up I could tell that he was mad

I got on it so quick that he didn't have time to fuss

I brought him to the edge again but I still wouldn't let him bust

I almost didn't stop in time that was a close call

I stood up and told him now I want you to take me up against the wall

He looked so tired his legs were shaking as he stood

But he wouldn't back down my stuff was too good

He picked me up and I wrapped my legs around him tight

And made him glad once again that he had brought me home that night

He didn't want to cum standing up so he carried me back to the bed

I put my legs up on his shoulders and crossed my feet behind his head

I told him to go deeper so the neighbors would know his name

But that this was one Karmel cat that he would never tame

His strokes got faster and he came with a shout

And after that big boy was Knocked Out

Be My

Be my Romeo and I'll be your Juliette
Without all of the fighting and other crazy shit
Well except for the naked wrestling and tongue fights
Which you will look forward to every single night

Or you can be my Lancelot and I'll be your Guinevere
You don't need shining armor just bring your lance here
Be my king for the night and I'll be your whore
Don't worry about chivalry leave me breathless and sore

Or I can be Cleopatra and you my Marc Antony
Be my gladiator sheath your sword in me
No need to go to war no need for suicide
Although I do need you to lay back so I can ride

I can be Hester Prynne and you Rev. Dimmesdale
We can do things worthy of a timeless tale
I want you to make me say your name
I will wear your mark proudly with no shame

Be my Mr. Darcy I'll be your Elizabeth
We will make the kind of love you won't easily forget
I promise to swallow more than my pride
If you'll let me take your body for a ride

You can be my Adam and I can be your Eve
We can go in the garden and make love among the leaves
We can become one body from these hot two
Because right now your rib isn't the bone I want from you

I'll be Bathsheba and you can be King David and stare
No need to sneak around we can do it anywhere
You can watch me dance I'll put on a private show
Then I'll play with your soldier stroke him nice and slow

Be my Solomon and I'll be your concubine
Let me do things that make you feel better than wine
I'll do things to set your body free
Make you wonder why you didn't marry me

I can be Esther and you can be my king
I just need one night to make your body sing
After I'm done showing you how I get down
I promise you won't mind sharing your crown

You can be my quill and I'll be your scroll
Please write the words that touch my soul
Use your skills to make an impression
Mark me with a timeless lesson

You can be Winston and help me get my groove back
Show me the skills my other lovers lacked
Bless me with your youthful endurance
I don't want this to be a one-time occurrence

I can be Maggie and you can be my Brick
Live up to your name I like it hard and thick
I don't care if the walls are thick or thin
I want you right now so let's get it in

I'll be your Janie if you'll be my Teacake
Make others jealous with the love that we make
Run your fingers through my hair
While saying my name and taking me there

You can be my mystery I'll be Agatha Christie
Let me write on you with every drop of ink in me
Let me build you up then bring you back down
Answer the question of all those nightly sounds

You can be the book that I read often
Learning the ways to make your hardness soften
Teach me the things you need me to try
I will happily decipher your pages if you just be my

www.ingramcontent.com/pod-product-compliance
Lightning Source LLC
Chambersburg PA
CBHW031203090426
42736CB00009B/766